# Telican Pelica

# A Bird's-Eye View of What to Do in Vero Beach

written and illustrated by Ardith M. Schneider

## Contents

A portion of the proceeds from this book will be donated to the Environmental Learning Center.

## Differences Between Pelicans

Brown

White

"Telican" is my name
And touring is my aim.
I love to show visitors what to do.
Actually, I'm a visitor too.
*Snowbirds* get their name from me.
In the Fall - down South I flee.
Around the country I migrate and roam
While my brown relative stays at home.
He also plunge-dives for his fish;
That's a skill for which I wish.
I float around and use my scoop.
White pelicans herd fish in a group.
We concentrate the fish just so
And gobble them up before they go.
You see, we two differ quite a lot;
We're more social and they are not.
That's why I'm guiding you to sights-
There are so many Indian River delights!

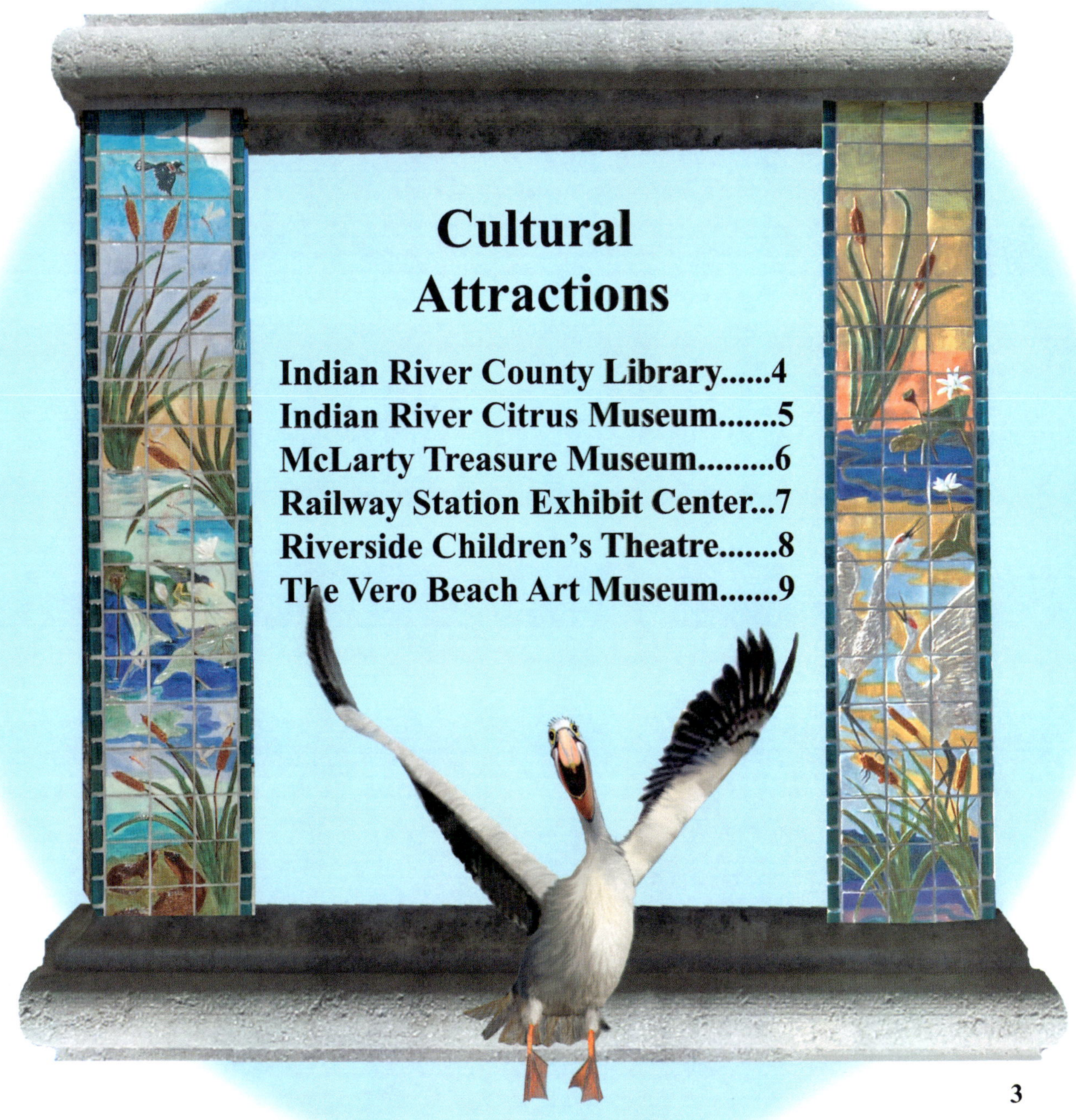

# Cultural Attractions

This library is really neat.
It even has a book called *Pelican Pete.*
It has books, programs, and DVDs,
All you have to do is say *Please.*
Signing up for a library card is so fast;
Your knowledge will become quite vast!

For more information see p. 46.

Now here's a good place to stop -
It's a museum about our citrus crop.
You'll learn about the orange and clementine
And other fruits from the state of sunshine.

For more information see p. 46.

**When you have a little leisure,**
**Be sure to go to the museum of treasure!**
**Here's where I learned to boast**
**Of why we're called *The Treasure Coast.***
**You can find out about the sunken ships**
**And why they went to Spain on trips!**

**For more information see p. 46.**

For more information see p. 46.

Whoopie!
Live children's theatre is right here in Vero,
From Peter Rabbit to a folktale hero!
You can watch a performance by your peers
Or work backstage to explore new frontiers.
RIVERSIDE THEATRE
For more information see p. 46.
8

## The Vero Beach Museum of Art

The art museum is a great place to go,
Paintings galore and bronze animals you might know.
If you like to paint, draw or create,
Their classes for kids are really first-rate!

For more information see p. 46

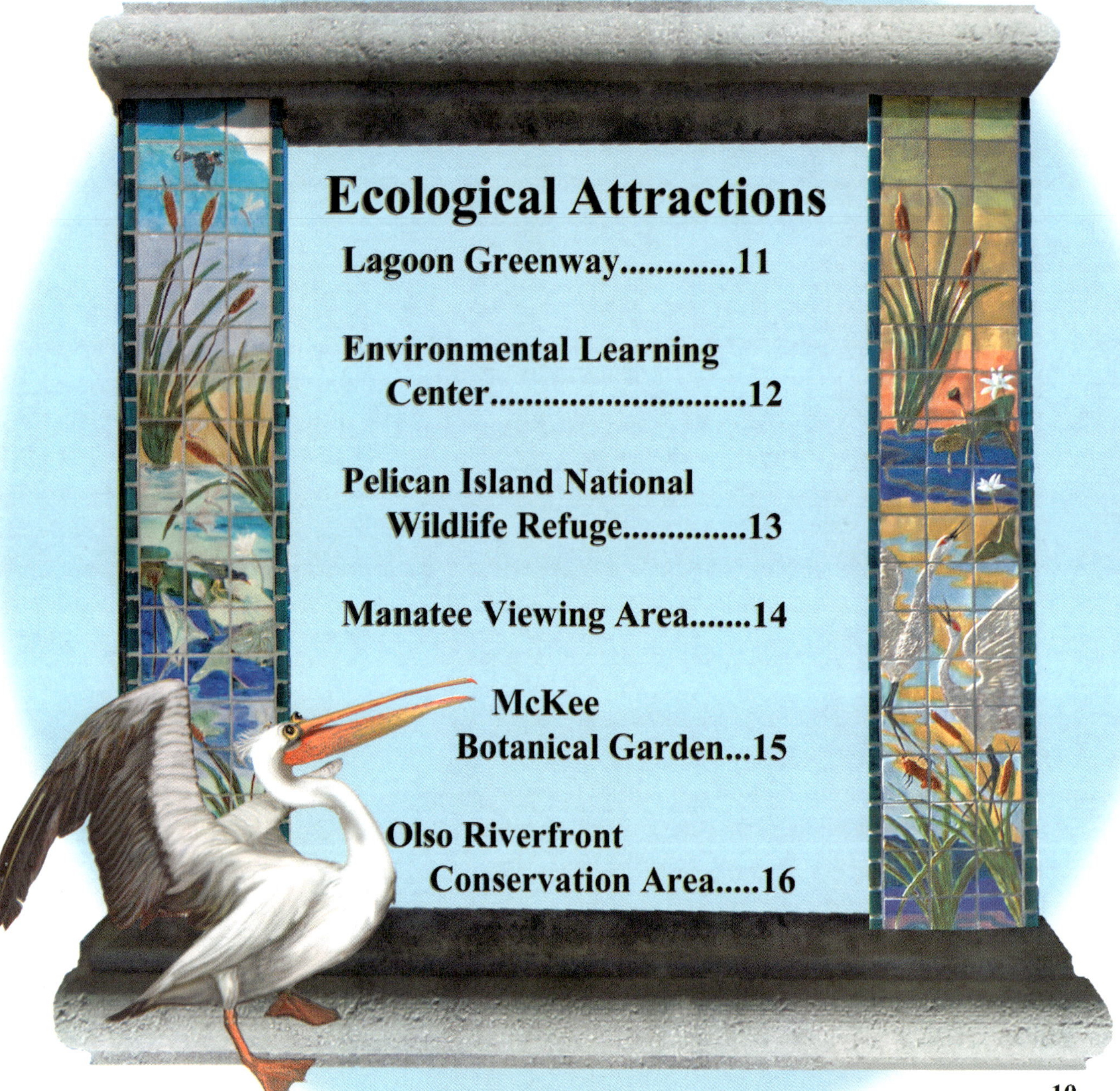

# Ecological Attractions

Yippee, another trail to hike.
It says right here you can even bike.
I've got the map with me -
We can start off by the big palm tree.
You might even hear me squawk
As we go about our 3-mile walk.
KEEP DOGS ON LEASH
For more information on the Lagoon Greenway see p. 47
Courtesy of the Indian River Land Trust

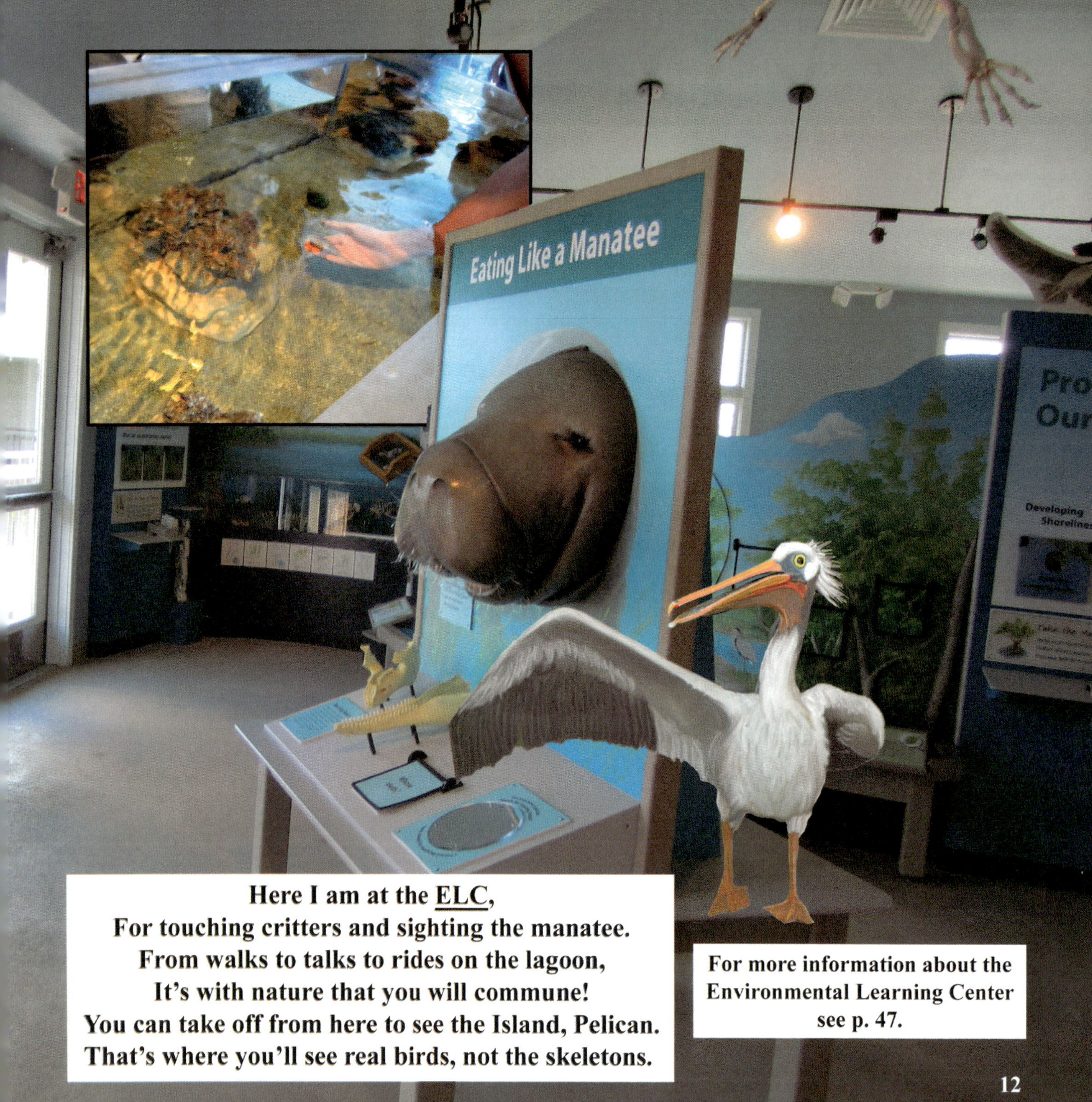


Here I am at the <u>ELC</u>,
For touching critters and sighting the manatee.
From walks to talks to rides on the lagoon,
It's with nature that you will commune!
You can take off from here to see the Island, Pelican.
That's where you'll see real birds, not the skeletons.

For more information about the Environmental Learning Center see p. 47.

**Pelican Island** is where we birds just blossom.
So many white pelicans - it's awesome!
Big bill and a 9-foot wing span,
My brothers are an impressive clan!
They stay in Vero all winter long,
Seeing old friends and growing strong.
Toward the end of March, off they go;
They've had a nice vacation in Vero!

For more information see p. 47.

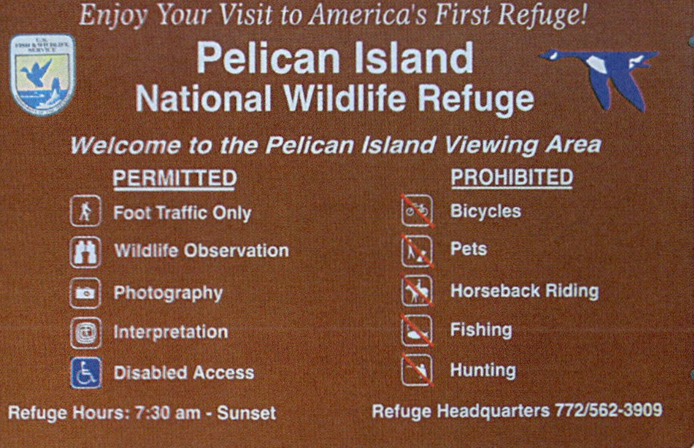

**Go to where the manatees hang out;**
**Then look carefully to see the snout.**
**Next to the 17th St. Bridge Power Plant,**
**These mammals are sure to enchant!**

Manatee Viewing Area

For more information see p. 47.

For more information see p. 47

Here's a riverfront area not to ignore,
Where you can hike, jog and explore.
With many canals and paths to stride,
Bring an area map as a guide.
There's a lake with a long lookout
And rustic trails for a good scout.
One bird you just might spy
Is a roseate spoonbill in the sky.

Oslo Riverfront Conservation Area (ORCA)
For more information see p. 47.

## Attractions: North & South

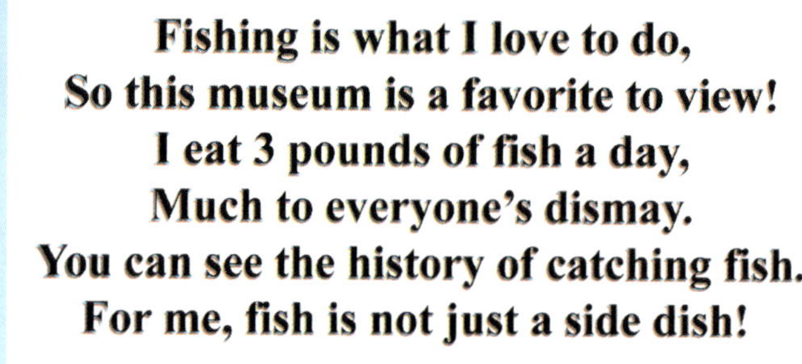

Fishing is what I love to do,
So this museum is a favorite to view!
I eat 3 pounds of fish a day,
Much to everyone's dismay.
You can see the history of catching fish.
For me, fish is not just a side dish!

The Fishing Museum, Sebastian

For more information see p. 48.

**_Tia_ the turtle greets you at the door,**
**Of this new museum with exhibits galore.**
**There are so many things for kids to do,**
**So just step right in and try a few.**
**You can't miss this building over the line**
**Right at the _Barrier Island Sanctuary_ sign.**

**For more information on The Barrier Island Center see p. 48.**

Although we never get a rainy day,
Here's an amazing museum on A1A.
Just south of Vero you will see
The Navy SEAL Museum and the UDT.
That stands for *Underwater Demolition Team*.
Those frogmen serve in conditions most extreme.

For more information see p. 48.

**Once you visit, you will agree**
**There's so much to learn about**
**the deep, deep sea.**
**They are farming tilapia in the back.**
**For things to see and do, there is no lack!**
**You can even buy a cookbook just for the lionfish**
**And surprise your family with an unusual dish!**

**For more information about Harbor Branch Ocean Discovery Center see p. 48.**

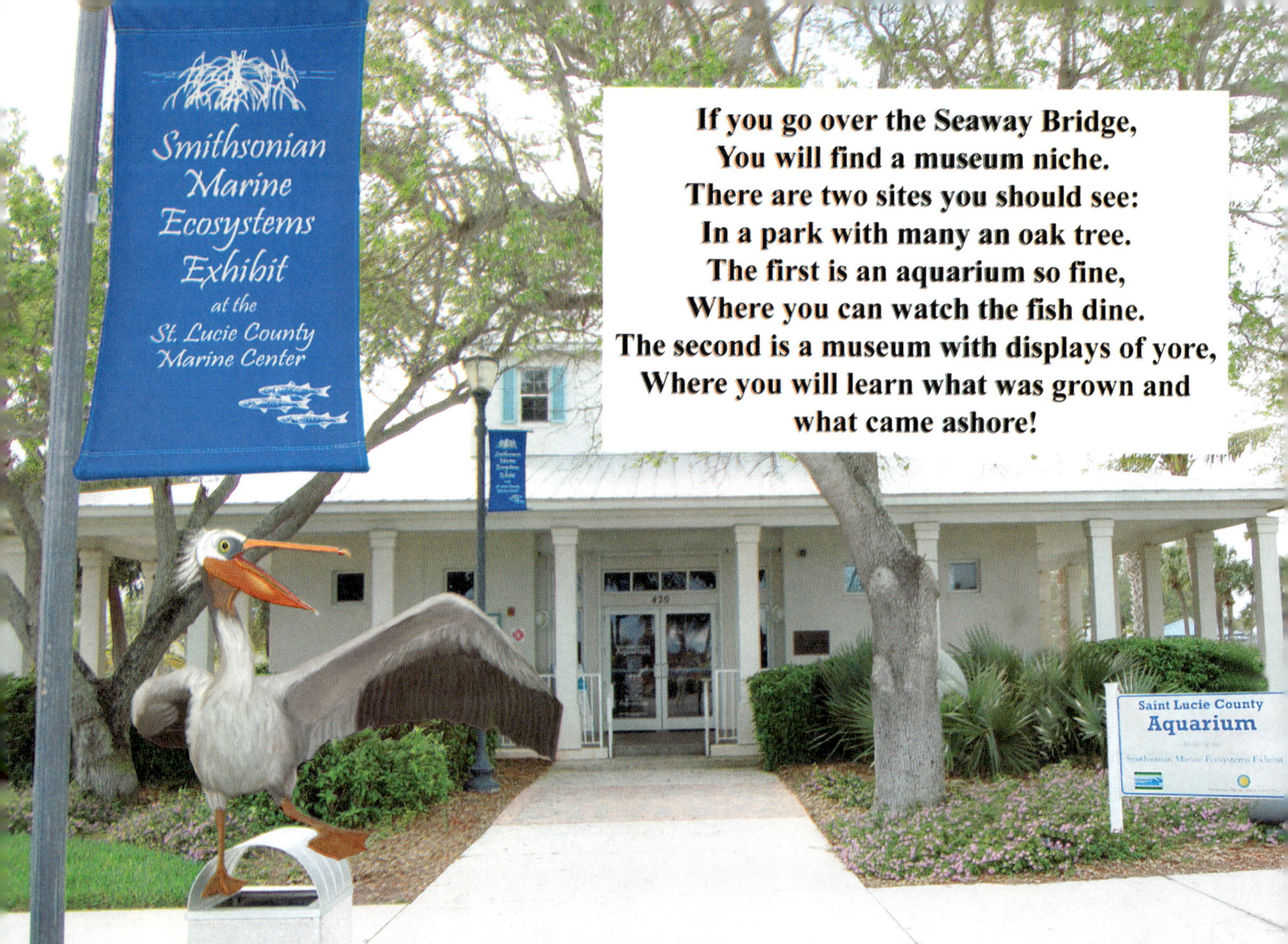

**If you go over the Seaway Bridge,**
**You will find a museum niche.**
**There are two sites you should see:**
**In a park with many an oak tree.**
**The first is an aquarium so fine,**
**Where you can watch the fish dine.**
**The second is a museum with displays of yore,**
**Where you will learn what was grown and what came ashore!**

**An easy walk from the Aquarium, past the playground to the - Regional History Center**

**For more information see p. 48.**

**Here's a place that is so worthwhile**
**Although it's quite south on the barrier isle.**
**You can learn about turtles and skates.**
**For marine life it's a museum first-rate.**
**Across the street is a treasure supreme;**
**Let your mind soar - that's the theme.**
**The Elliott Museum is about originality**
**and the American dream.**

For more information see p. 49.

Here's a place that is so worthwhile
Although it's quite south on the barrier isle.
You can learn about turtles and skates.
For marine life it's a museum first-rate.
Across the street is a treasure supreme;
Let your mind soar - that's the theme.
The Elliott Museum is about originality
and the American dream.

For more information see p. 49.

# Parks

## Indian River Parks



## Inland Parks



## Ocean Beach Parks

**Here you have an unparalled view,**
**Of the lagoon and two bridges, too!**
**A place for picnics and quiet play,**
**Watching boats, pelicans and osprey.**
**And, just in case you want to know,**
**A.W. Young was the first mayor of Vero!**

For more information on A.W. Young Park see p. 49.

**Here's a park to go to next.**
**It even has a baseball complex.**
**There's a boat ramp and a dog park too,**
**Good to explore before you're through!**
**You see the Barber Bridge afar,**
**And you know just where you are!**

**For more information see page 49.**

*Bark in the Park* is one big deal.
Where dogs try their best to pose and heel.
The field at the park is really ideal -
For both owners and onlookers,
This event really appeals.

For more information on
Riverside Park see p. 49.

So much goes on at this park so fine.
There are separate areas by design.
You can play tennis, jog or walk -
Even watch a blue heron on a rock.
Veterans Island is at the large flag,
Where you can see the squirrels play tag.
There are events here from dusk til dawn,
Surprising sights you'll come upon!

The Grand Pavilion

For more information see p. 49.

**What fun to climb up high and see,**
**The very tops of many a tree.**
**An adventure you would certainly agree.**
**There's a bridge to get to this place;**
**You can walk or jog or race.**
**But be careful not to trip**
**As there are many roots quite thick.**

**For more information see p. 49.**

## Royal Palm Pointe Park

I love to jump off this weathered pine,
and then dry off in the bright sunshine.
I see the children getting wet
In the fountains - they won't forget.
They'll ask again and again,
Can we go to Royal Palm Pointe
not just *now and then*?

For more information see p. 49.

**If acrobatics is your skill,**
**Then Leisure Square will fill the bill.**
**This facility was once a YMCA,**
**Winners are here - trophies on display.**
**You can learn to be quite a champ,**
**By attending Circus Summer Camp.**
**Swimming, rugby and jujitsu too,**
**So many activities to pursue!**

**For more information see p. 49.**

**Named after a Native American lass,**
**<u>Pocahontas Park</u> is really first class.**
**Little cars on which to ride -**
**Down you go on many a slide.**
**Right on 14th Avenue, by the way;**
**What a wonderful place to play!**

**For more information see p. 49.**

Find out where these park are on p. 49.

For more information see p. 50

I'm about to disembark,
From a slide in Jaycee Park.
Conn Beach is right beyond the trees,
Lifeguards are here, as well as the breeze.
There's the Sunset Grill to get a snack,
In case a lunch you forgot to pack.

For more information see p. 50.

**Back I go to the ocean's brine.**
**This beach is on the county line.**
**See the Atlantic's whitecaps swell**
**On <u>Round Island Beach</u> as well.**
**Also, heed the warnings posted,**
***Safety here* I've always boasted.**

**For more information see p. 50.**

May I present to you <u>South Beach</u>,
Right in the middle, so easy to reach.
Lifeguards aplenty right on site,
For swimmers, sunbathers and
even a kite!

For more information see p. 50.

Checking off beaches up the line,
Tracking Station is a great one to find.
I see a red flag peeking out.
Do you remember what that flag is about?
There are two more beaches going north -
Golden Sands and Treasure Shores.
What a wealth of sand and sun.
This Vero Beach cannot be outdone!

For more information see p. 50.

# Fairs, Festivals, Fishing and Boat Rides

**March is the time for**
**The <u>IRC Firefighters' Fair</u>.**
**You will see sights beyond compare.**
**The 4-H is showing prize cows**
**While among the booths you browse.**
**Food, rides and contests too,**
**This event is the thing to do!**
**You'll learn about fire prevention too!**

**For more information see p. 51.**

With a beautiful title and sunny weather,
For this event the city really comes together.
Every April for more than a decade,
This family festival has seen many an upgrade.
Now it is established so well,
Everyone attending thinks it's swell!
Over 10,000 went last year.
It's not near the water, but I will appear!

# Hibiscus Festival

For more information see p. 51.

Here's a nice safe place to fish
Right under the Barber bridge.
You can't fall in because there's a rail,
And don't worry about catching a whale.
You'll also see kayaks on the H2O;
It's part salt and part fresh, you know.

For more information see p. 51.

**There are so many trips to take by boat,**
**From kayaks to a pontoon.**
**See the sunset and then the moon**
**And all the creatures on the lagoon!**

**For more information see p. 51.**

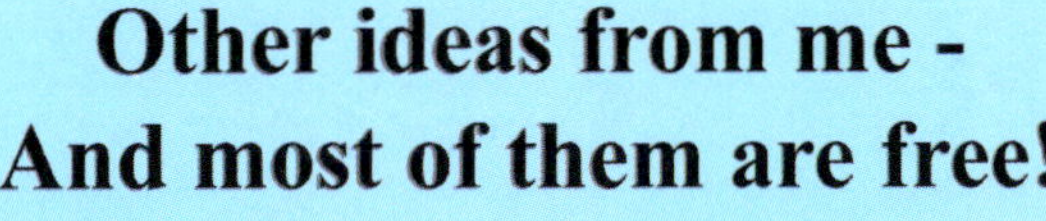

# Other ideas from me -
# And most of them are free!

Fly a kite.

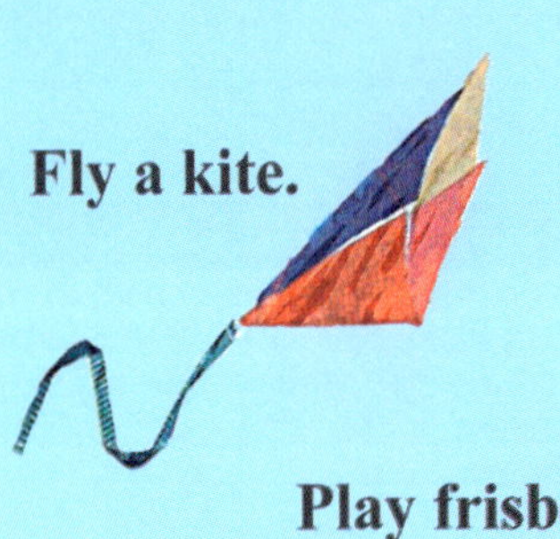

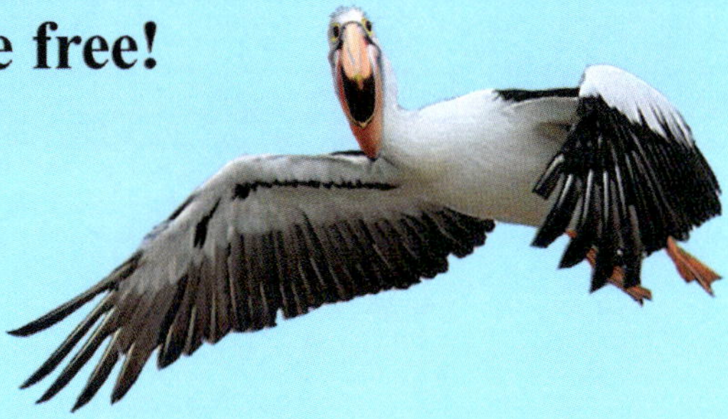

Play frisbee.

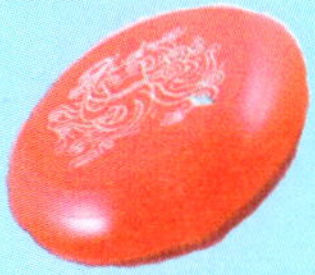

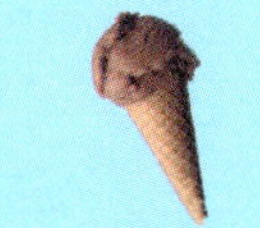

Eat ice cream.

Get some bait for fishing.

Listen to an author speak.

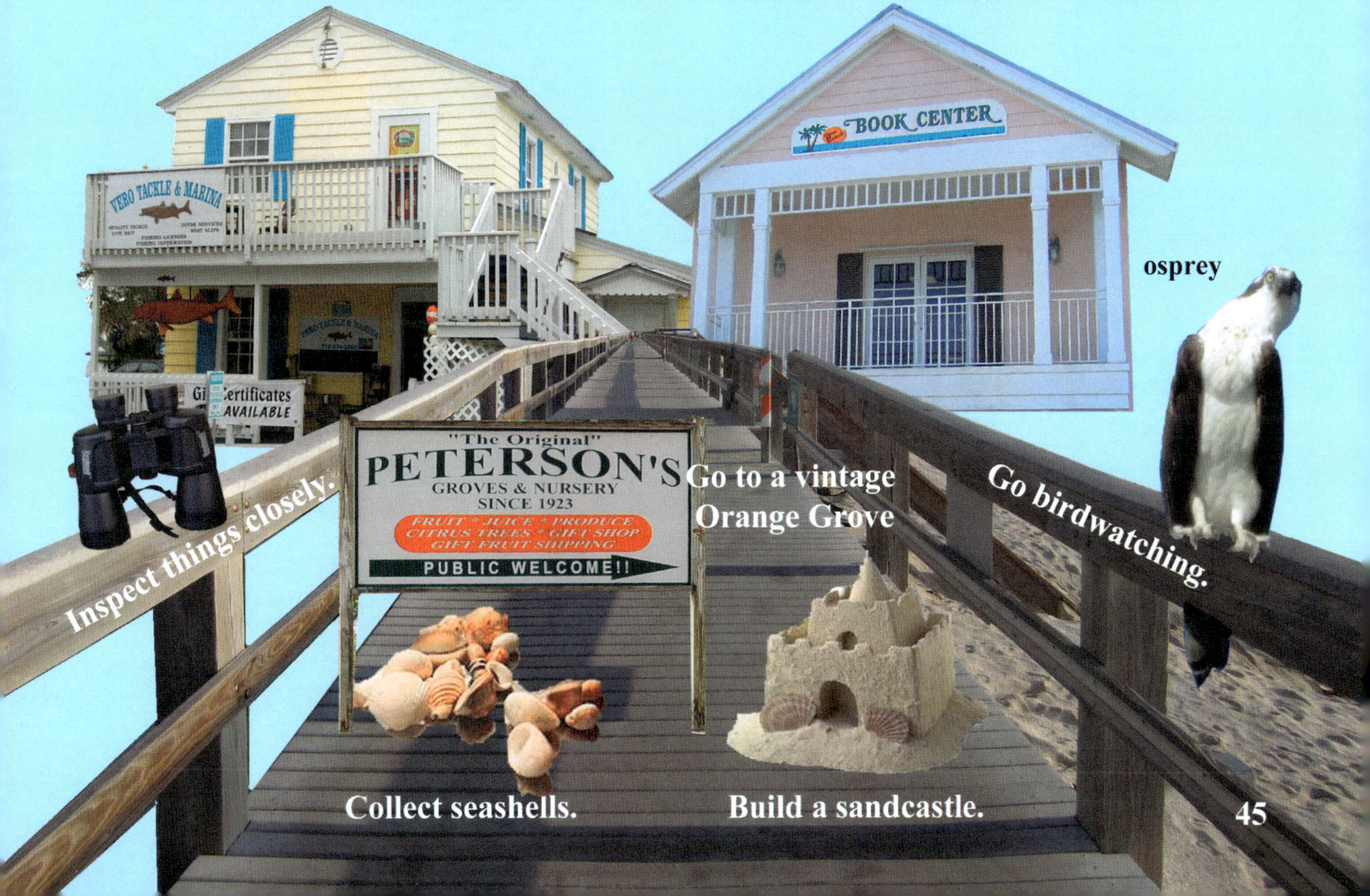

VERO TACKLE & MARINA
Gift Certificates AVAILABLE
BOOK CENTER
"The Original"
PETERSON'S
GROVES & NURSERY
SINCE 1923
FRUIT * JUICE * PRODUCE
CITRUS TREES * GIFT SHOP
GIFT FRUIT SHIPPING
PUBLIC WELCOME!!


osprey

Inspect things closely.

Go to a vintage Orange Grove

Go birdwatching.

Collect seashells.

Build a sandcastle.

More information on sights to see, places to go and events in Vero Beach on these *www* **sites**: cultural-council.com, indianriverchamber.com, verobeach.com, covb.org, mainstreetverobeach.org, gotoverobeach.com, verobeachflash.com, indianriverlagoonbyway.com and comediscovernature.com, and don't forget to read *Vero Beach 32963* and the *Indian River Press Journal* for calendar listings.

**INDEX - CULTURAL**

(Addresses are in Vero Beach unless indicated, attractions are free unless noted and see website for hours of operation.)

**Indian River County Library,** 1600 21st St., 772-770-5060, www.IRCLibrary.org. The library's collection consists of over 270,000 items including books, magazines, newspapers, CDs, audio books, DVDs and eBooks. Entertaining educational programs for children are numerous.

**Indian River Citrus Museum,** 2140 14th Ave. (to the left of The Heritage Center), 772-770-2263, www.veroheritage.org/citrusmuseum.html. This small museum exhibits artifacts relating to the history of the citrus industry.

**McLarty Treasure Museum,** 13180 N. SR A1A, 772-589-2147, www.atocha1622.com/mclarty.htm. The museum offers displays of treasure taken from the ships that went down in the hurricane of 1715, plus a 45-minute video of the history and salvaging efforts. Admission is $2.00 per person, children under 6 admitted free. (Fishing Museum and Turtle Museum are just 2 miles and 5 miles north respectively).

**Railway Station Exhibit Center**, 2336 14th Ave., 772-778-3435, www.irchistorical.org, >Properties. This small museum is housed in the first railway station. There are many photographs and displays including an electric train making the journey through the old towns of Fellsmere and Vero Beach (pictured on page 7).

**Riverside Children's Theatre (RCT),** 3280 Riverside Park Drive, 772-231-6990. www.riversidetheatre.com/riverside_childrens_theatre.php. RCT is the educational and youth-orientated arm of the Riverside Theatre. After school and summer instruction in performing arts are conducted with in-house productions.

**The Vero Beach Museum of Art,** 3001 Riverside Park Dr., 772-231-0707, www.verobeachmuseum.org. Besides art exhibits presenting important American and international works of art, there are classes for children of all ages – Family Fun Shops and Summer Art Camp. A Children's Art Festival is held annually in April. Red sculpture shown on page 9 is Trevan's Arch, by Haydn Llewellyn Davies, Canadian, born Wales (1921-2008), 1978, Brakeform aluminum 30 x 24 x 18 feet, Museum Purchase with funds provided by Susan K. Mallinson. "Trial Scene," 1997 by American artist, Thomas Otterness, Bronze (Edition 5 of 6). Collection of The Vero Beach Museum of Art purchased through funds provided by the Mr. & Mrs. Robert L. Stott, Jr. Acquisition Fund.

## INDEX – ECOLOGICAL ATTRACTIONS

**Lagoon Greenway,** Indian River Blvd. and 8th St., 772-794-0701, www.indianriverlandtrust.org. There are three trails: Main Trail (under ½ mile), Mini-adventure Trail (1/4 mile loop, no bicycles on this one) and the Two-mile Loop Trail. Maps available at the parking lot. See the website for free conservation tours at the 4 other land trust acquisitions.

**Environmental Learning Center (ELC),** 225 Live Oak Dr., (1.4 miles west of the Wabasso traffic light), 772-589-5050, www.discoverelc.org, This 64-acre sanctuary and non-profit center includes a nature nook, discovery center, touch tank, aquarium, butterfly garden, hiking, canoeing and pontoon boat rides. EcoVentures abound for children and families. Admission Fee: $5/person, children under 12 free and first Saturday of the month is free to all. See website for hours, closed Mondays.

**Pelican Island National Wildlife Refuge**, 4 miles North of CR 510 off on A1A, 772-581-5557, www.fws.gov/pelicanisland. Established in 1903, this island (3 acres) attracts over 130 bird species annually. The refuge (over 5400 acres of upland habitat in close proximity to Pelican Island proper) offers free wildlife tours, guided bird walks, butterfly tours and more. Organizations, like the ELC, offer boat/kayak/canoe trips around the island. No one is actually allowed on the island.

**Manatee Viewing Area**, On Indian River Blvd., next to the Vero Beach Power Plant and the 17th St. bridge. Visitors can drive in the parking area and walk a short distance north to a small viewing area. Manatees enjoy the warmer water of the canal and can usually be spotted here.

**McKee Botanical Garden,** 350 US Highway 1, 772-794-0601, www.mckeegarden.org. This subtropical jungle hammock (closed canopy forest) is an 18-acre site with trails and architectural treasures to be explored. Guided tours, maps, classes, events, Garden Discovery Backpacks and summer camp for children are available. Admission Fee: $10/person, Seniors: $9, Children (3-12): $5.00, Under 3: Free. These rates are for October 31st to April 30th. Rates slightly lower between May 1st and October 30. Garden is open: Tuesday – Saturday 10 – 5 and Sunday: noon -5.

**Oslo Riverfront Conservation Area (ORCA),** 772-589-9223, www.floridahikes.com/osloriverfront. East of US 1 on Oslo Road, CR 606, (look for sign on the left), Rustic trails, observation towers and platform at ORCA are open to the public from dawn to dusk daily. For this adventurous hike you should have a map, cell phone and mosquito repellent. Bird sighting opportunities abound. The area is managed by Indian River County.

## INDEX – ATTRACTIONS: NORTH AND SOUTH

**North – Sebastian Fishing Museum,** 9700 South State Road A1A, 321-984-4852, www.floridastateparks.org/sebastianinlet/ The museum is devoted to the rich cultural history of the Sebastian fishing industry. Inside are many displays including a replica of a vintage fishing house and a dock. Museum is open 7 days a week from 10 to 4.

**Barrier Island Center,** 8385 S.Hwy. A1A, Melbourne Beach, 321-723-3556 www.conserveturtles.org/barrierislandcenter.php This museum is an educational center located in the heart of the **Archie Carr Refuge**, a major nesting site for sea turtles about 3 miles North of the Sebastian Inlet Bridge on A1A. The refuge was created to protect the habitats of the loggerhead sea turtle and the green turtle. At this center, there are many unique hands-on exhibits for children. The Archie Carr National Wildlife Refuge spans a total of over 20 linear miles along the coast in this area. There are **turtle walks** in June and July, contact 321-984-4852 at Sebastian Inlet State Park. Hours are: Tuesday – Sunday, 9 – 5.

**South – Fort Pierce National Navy UDT/SEAL Museum,** 3300 North A1A, 772-595-5845, www.navysealmuseum.com. This attraction is dedicated solely to preserving the history of the Navy SEALs and their predecessors. Fort Pierce is the birthplace of the Navy Frogmen. Hours are: Tuesday – Saturday 10 – 4, Sunday: 12 – 4. Admission: Adults (13 and over) $8., Children (6-12) $4., Children 5 and under: Free. Group rates available.

**Ocean Discovery Center (Harbor Branch),** 5600 US 1, 772-242-2417, www.fau.edu/hboi/OceanDiscoveryCenter.php. The center is the public gateway to Harbor Branch Oceanographic Institute at Florida Atlantic University. There are interactive exhibits, small aquaria, a video theater and other displays. Hours are: Monday – Friday, 10 – 5, Saturday, 10 – 2.

**Smithsonian Marine Ecosystems Exhibit**, 420 Seaway Drive, Fort Pierce, 772-462-3474, www.sms.si.edu/SMEE/index.htm. The focus of this aquarium is on displaying ecosystems as complex communities of organisms interacting in their environment. Hours are: Tues. – Sat., 10 -4, Sunday, 12 to 4. Admission: Adults: $4, seniors: $3, children (4-17): $3.**Regional History Center,** 414 Seaway Drive, Fort Pierce, 772-462-1795, www.stlucieco.gov/history/index.htm. This museum gives a glimpse at the foundations of Fort Pierce from the Ais Indians, Creeks and Seminoles to the 1900s. It also features sunken treasures, artifacts from turn-of-the-century industries and many other displays. Hours are: Wednesday – Saturday, 10 – 4, Sunday 12 – 4.

**Manatee Observation and Education Center,** 480 N. Indian River Dr., Fort Pierce, 772-429-6266, www.manateecenter.com. The Manatee Center has displays and hands-on exhibits including informative computer programs. Experience the diversity of the Indian River Lagoon with an educational Wildlife Boat Tour, or a guided kayak adventure. Hours are: Tuesday – Saturday, 10 – 5, Sunday 12 – 4 (October 1 – June 30). Off-season Thurs. – Sat., 10 – 5. Admission: $1.00 per person, children under 5 admitted free.

## INDEX – ATTRACTIONS: SOUTH OF FORT PIERCE AND PARKS

**Fort Pierce Power Plant, Educational Tours,** (not pictured in book) *Energy Encounter*, 6501S. Ocean Dr., Jensen Beach, 1-877-FPL-4FUN, www.fpl.com.

**Florida Oceanographic & Coastal Center,** 890 NE Ocean Blvd., Stuart, 772-225-0505, www.floridaocean.org. The Coastal Center provides a natural learning environment through its interactive exhibits on mammals, fish and sea turtles. Of note are the stingray pavilion, the game fish lagoon and the nature trail. Hours are: Monday – Saturday, 10 – 5, Sunday 12 – 4. Admission: Adults $10.00, Children 3 to 12 years $5.00, under 3 admitted free.

**The Elliott Museum** (not pictured in book), 825 NE Ocean Blvd. Stuart, 772-225-1961, www.elliottmuseumfl.org. The newly rebuilt and revisioned Elliott Museum will focus on art, history and technology. Hours are: Monday – Sunday 10 – 5, Admission: Adults $12.00, seniors $10.00, children 2 – 12 years $6.00, under 2 admitted free.

### PARKS – INDIAN RIVER PARKS

**Information on City Parks:** www.covb.org **>City Departments >Recreation> City Parks Information**

**A.W. Young Park**, 21st Street east of Indian River Blvd. (sign on Indian River Blvd says "Park Ave."). This scenic park on the lagoon has views of the two Vero Beach bridges, picnic areas, grills, restrooms and fishing.

**MacWilliam Park**, Indian River Drive East, north of east end of the Barber Bridge, *On-Leash* Dog Park, 772-231-0809.

**Riverside Park (2 pages)**, Riverside Drive, off Mockingbird Drive, south of east end of the Barber Bridge, Veterans Memorial Island Sanctuary is an island off the main park. 772-231-4787. Riverside Racquet Complex (10 tennis courts). *Bark in the Park,* sponsored by the Humane Society of Vero Beach is just one of the many events held in Riverside Park.

**Round Island Riverside Park**, 2201 A1A, west side, near Indian River/St. Lucie line. Park features: boat launch, picnic tables, grills, restrooms, boardwalk, bridge and observation tower (pictured in book), 772-492-2412.

**Royal Palm Pointe Park**, 2 Royal Palm Pointe, 772-567-2144, Park features: scenic views, picnic tables, restrooms, fishing dock and an "interactive" fountain. Normal fountain hours: 10 – 3, Wednesday through Saturday. Call for holiday hours.

**INLAND PARKS: Leisure Square**, 3705 16th Street, 772-770-6500, Leisure Square features: picnic tables, grills, swimming pool, playground, basketball, indoor racquetball, volleyball, acrobatics and gymnastics. Fee required.

**Pocahontas Park**, 21st Street and 14th Avenue, Extensive play areas for children, tennis courts, picnic tables and restrooms.

**Neighborhood Parks: Jacoby Park,** 19th Street and 25th Avenue**; Piece of Pie Park,** 37th Avenue and Atlantic Blvd., Restrooms; **Charles Park,** 15th Street and 24th Avenue, Restrooms; **Troy Moody Park**, Victory Blvd. and Cordova Avenue.

## INDEX - OCEAN BEACH PARKS

**Humiston Park,** 901 Ocean Drive at Dahlia Lane, 772-231-5790, Park features: boardwalk, fishing, grills, picnic areas, playground, restrooms and outdoor showers. Lifeguards are on duty from 10 to 3 daily.

**Jaycee Park (adjacent to Conn Beach),** 4200-4400 Ocean Drive, 772-231-0578, Park features a beach wheelchair, boardwalk, fishing, grills, picnic areas, playground, beach volleyball, restrooms and outdoor showers. Lifeguards are on duty 9 to 5. Not pictured in book: **Bethel Creek Park** (across Ocean Drive from Jaycee Park), 4405 SR A1A, Park features: fishing, grills, picnic areas and restrooms.

**Round Island Park**, 2200 S. A1A, (Indian River/St. Lucie County line), 772-492-2412, Park features: picnic areas, grills, pavilions, boardwalk, restrooms, showers and ADA crossover area. Lifeguards are on duty from 9:10 – 4:50.

**South Beach Park**, 1704 Ocean Drive, end of East Causeway (17th Street Bridge), 772-231-4700, Park features: a beach wheelchair, boardwalk, fishing, grills, picnic areas, playground, beach volleyball, restrooms and outdoor showers. Lifeguards on duty from 9 – 5.

**Tracking Station Park**, 800 46th Place E, off North A1A, Entrance between CVS Pharmacy and the 7-11 Store. Park features: picnic areas, grills, restrooms and showers. Lifeguards are on duty from 9:10 to 4:50. Hours are sunrise to sunset.

## PUBLIC ACCESS BEACHES

**Riomar Beach Access:** Ocean Drive, south of Beachland Boulevard; **Seagrape Trail:** A1A south of Wabasso Beach; **Turtle Trail**: A1A north of Old Winter Park Road; **Sexton Plaza**: east of Beachland Boulevard at Ocean Drive intersection.

### Other Ocean Beaches on North A1A

**Wabasso Beach Park,** 1808 Wabasso Beach Rd., east of A1A intersection and north of Disney Resort, 772-581-4998.

**Golden Sands Beach Park,** A1A 1.4 miles north of CR 510 (Wabasso), 772-581-4995.

**Treasure Shores Park,** 11300 A1A, three miles north of CR 510, 772-581-4997 (unguarded beach).

**Sebastian Inlet State Park**, 9700 A1A about 7 miles north of CR 510 intersection, 321-984-4852. Park features: camping, fishing, bait shop, nature walks, boardwalk, restrooms, and an excellent surfing site.

## INDEX – FAIRS, FESTIVALS, FISHING AND BOAT RIDES

**Firefighters' Fair,** www.firefightersfair.org. The Firefighters' Indian River County Fair has been an institution for over 30 years. It is an annual 10-day event which includes: a Fire Fighting Training Show, food, 4-H livestock barn, spectacular rides, carnival games, demolition derby and strolling entertainment. The fair takes place early in March.

**Hibiscus Festival,** www.hibiscusfestival.org, www.mainstreetverobeach.org. This annual mid-April festival is sponsored by Main Street Vero Beach, a group of residents dedicated to promote civic pride and community involvement in the downtown historic area. This popular event includes: a 5K run, juried fine art show, marketplace, continuous musical entertainment, Miss Hibiscus pageant and activities celebrating Earth Day.

**Fishing Places,** www.verobeach.com, www.fishverobeach.com. Besides the area under the Merrill Barber Bridge, there are many parks in Vero where you can fish. These parks are listed in this index and you can see which ones permit fishing. A fishing license is not required until age 16. See website www.public.myfwc.com for details and free fishing days.

**Boating, Kayaking, Air Boat Rides,**

Once again www.verobeach.com is the starting point for these activities. By searching the Internet or the phone book you can find many sources for lagoon and swamp adventure. There are charters, rentals and sightseeing pontoon boats that go out from Vero Beach, Fort Pierce and Sebastian. The airboat rides are exciting as you are bound to see an alligator or two. Yes, up close and personal. Photo taken by Robert Schneider.

Below are kayakers at Round Island Park

## ACKNOWLEDGEMENTS

The idea for "Telican Pelican" germinated from conversations during water aerobics at The Moorings Club. While grandmothers were asking each other where to take their grandchildren, I was wondering what books were available on the subject of *things to do and see* in Vero Beach. I was unable to find such a book. Wow, what an opportunity!

It's been an amazing journey going to the various places in the book, taking photographs and talking to people at the sites. For a city of its size, Vero Beach and its neighboring towns have an imposing number of attractions, parks and events. It is evident that Vero's leadership is concerned about preserving the culture and conserving the environment. What a remarkable city to live in or visit!

**Susann Pezzetti and Cynthia Callander, Vero Beach Book Center; Allison McNeal, Indian River Chamber of Commerce; Sophie B. Wood, The Vero Beach Museum of Art; Oscar Sales and Heidi Waxlax, Riverside Children's Theatre; Christine Hobart, McKee Botanical Garden; Holly Dill, Environmental Learning Center; Jim Masterson, Harbor Branch Ocean Discovery Center; Laurie Lee, Vero Beach Parks Department; Amelia Graves, Hibiscus Festival; Toby Turner, Indian River County Firefighters' Fair, Ken Grudens, Executive Director, Indian River Land Trust; Debbie Avery, Cultural Council of Indian River County and all the pleasant and helpful staff members at the various entries in this book. (This list starts with first contacts, two years ago, to the present.) Editors: Special thanks go to Helen Jankoski and Liz Sayre for their assistance with grammar and idea clarification; last minute edits: Jim Morris and the McKernans. Thanks go to Joel Rockwell (pelican photo), my water aerobics class and many others for encouragement and suggestions.**

**Bee Gum Point** – Another trail to hike and a recent land acquisition by the Indian River Land Trust.

**About Potpourri (page 45)** – Although I steered away from mentioning commercial ventures, I couldn't help but add a few here. The Book Center has a separate Children's Store, 329 21st Street, www.theverobeachbookcenter.com. Vero Tackle & Marine is at 3321 Bridge Plaza Drive. Peterson's Grove is near the Indian River Mall at 3375 66th Street. It is a landmark and part of the citrus culture in Florida - lots to see including random animals.

**About the back cover**: *Turtle Trax* was a project created to benefit the Mental Health Association of Indian River County from 2005-2008. There are more than 30 in Vero.

Made in the USA
San Bernardino, CA
14 March 2014